GOODNIGHT TOMB

by Jeffrey Alan Williams

•

Pictures by Rose Nguyen

**In the dark zombie tomb
There was a girl, undead,
And a graveyard bed
And a picture of —**

A cat jumping over a head

And there was a shelf full of hearts and body parts

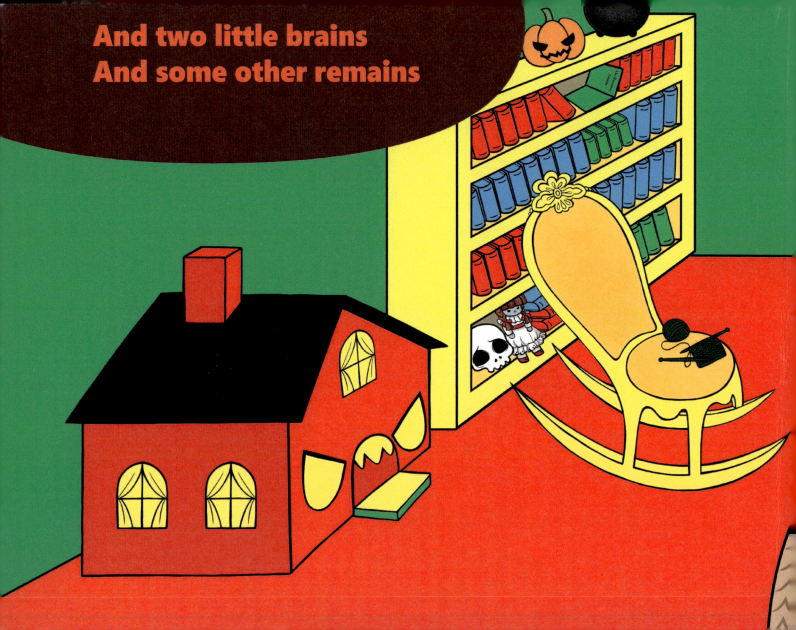

And some guts and a nose and a bowl full of toes

And an old lady beginning to decompose

Goodnight undead

Goodnight cat jumping over a head

Goodnight dark
And the graveyard bed

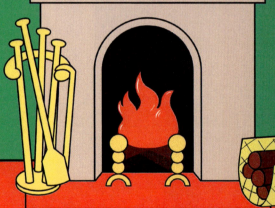

Goodnight hearts
Goodnight parts

Goodnight brains

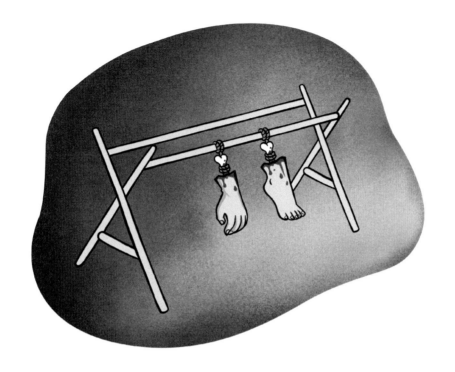

And goodnight remains

Goodnight groans

And goodnight moans

Goodnight nobody

Goodnight toes

Goodnight scare

Goodnight air

Made in the USA
Las Vegas, NV
24 October 2020